Weather

KINGFISHER

a Houghton Mifflin Company imprint
222 Berkeley Street
Boston, Massachusetts 02116
www.houghtonmifflinbooks.com

First published in 2006
2 4 6 8 10 9 7 5 3 1

1TR/0606/PRSP/RNB/140MA/F

LIBRARY OF CONGRESS CATALOGING-IN-PUBLICATION DATA
Savage, Stephen, 1965–
Weather/Stephen Savage.—1st ed.
p. cm.—(Kingfisher young knowledge)
Includes index.
ISBN-13: 978-0-7534-5983-6
ISBN-10: 0-7534-5983-3
1. Weather—Juvenile literature. I. Title. II. Series.
QC981.3.S28 2006
551.6—–dc22
2005033208

Senior editor: Vicky Bywater
Coordinating editor: Stephanie Pliakas
Designer: Joanne Brown
Cover designer: Poppy Jenkins
Picture research manager: Cee Weston-Baker
DTP manager: Nicky Studdart
DTP operator: Claire Cessford
Senior production controller: Jessamy Oldfield
Editor and indexer: Hannah Wilson

ISBN-13: 978-0-7534-5983-6
ISBN-10: 0-7534-5983-3

Printed in China

Acknowledgments
The publishers would like to thank the following for permission to reproduce their material. Every care has been
taken to trace copyright holders. However, if there have been unintentional omissions or failure to trace copyright
holders, we apologize and will, if informed, endeavor to make corrections in any future edition.
b = bottom, *c* = center, *l* = left, *t* = top, *r* = right

Phototgraphs: *cover* Taxi Getty; 1 Imagebank Getty; 2–3 A. & J. Verkalk Corbis; 4–5 Photonica Getty; 6*tr* Travelshots Alamy;
6*bl* Reportage Getty; 7 Don Mason Corbis; 8 Stone Getty; 9*tl* Nevada Weir Corbis; 9*r* Photolibrary.com; 10–11 Richard Cooke
Alamy; 11*tl* Simon Fraser Science Photo Library; 12–13 Taxi Getty; 12*cr* Imagebank Getty; 12*bl* Photographer's Choice Getty;
14–15 Still Pictures; 15*tl* Still Pictures; 15*cr* Mike Greenslade Alamy; 16–17 Roy Morsch Zefa Corbis; 16 Photolibrary.com; 18–19
Taxi Getty; 18*b* Remi Benali Corbis; 19*tr* Photolibrary.com; 20–21 Photographer's Choice Getty; 21 Stockbyte Platinum Getty;
22 National Geographic Society Getty; 23 Still Pictures; 23*tr* Pekka Parviainen Science Photo Library;
24–25 Photolibrary.com; 25*tl* Stone Getty; 25*br* Still Pictures; 26 Stone + Getty; 27*tl* Jim Reed Corbis; 27 Rick Wilking
Reuters Corbis; 28–29 Still Pictures; 29*tl* Still Pictures; 29*br* Iconica Getty; 30–31 Photographer's Choice Getty;
30*l* Photolibrary.com; 31 Iconica Getty; 32–33 Still Pictures; 33*t* Stone Getty; 33*b* Stone Getty; 34–35 Stone Getty;
35 Steve Bloom Alamy; 36–37 National Geographic Society Getty; 36*cr* Jim Reed Corbis; 36*bl* Masterfile; 38–39 Reportage
Getty; 38*bl* Getty Editorial; 39*br* Corbis; 40 Keren Su Corbis; 41*tl* Still Pictures; 41*br* Zute Lightfoot Alamy; 48 Taxi Getty

Commissioned photography on pages 42–47 by Andy Crawford
Project maker and photo shoot coordinator: Jo Connor
Thank you to models Dilvinder Dilan Bhamra, Cherelle Clarke, Madeleine Roffey, and William Sartin.

KFYK Kingfisher Young Knowledge

Weather

Caroline Harris

KINGFISHER
BOSTON

Contents

What is weather?   6

Our star   8

Blanket of air   10

Changing seasons   12

World climates   14

Blowing around   16

Wild wind   18

Blue planet   20

Mist and clouds   22

Out in the rain   24

Stormy days   26

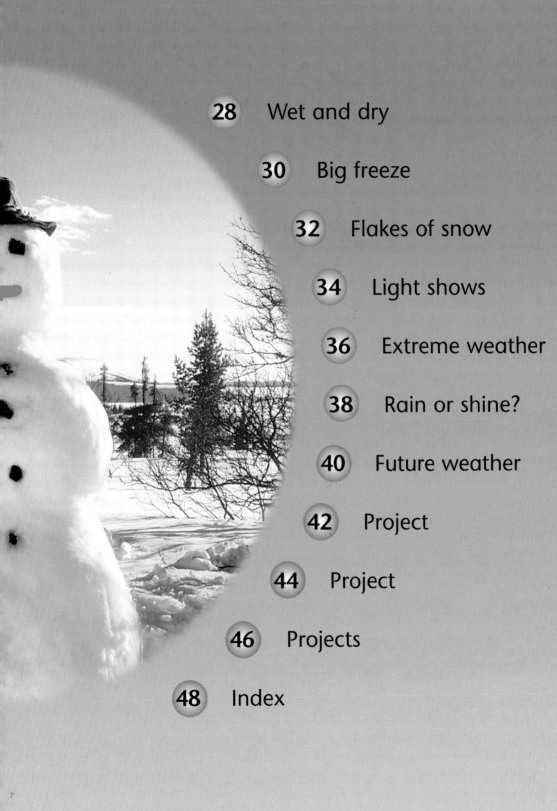

28 Wet and dry

30 Big freeze

32 Flakes of snow

34 Light shows

36 Extreme weather

38 Rain or shine?

40 Future weather

42 Project

44 Project

46 Projects

48 Index

What is weather?

Weather is all of the changes that happen in the air. Water, air, and heat from the Sun work together to make weather.

Warm and sunny

When the Sun is high in the sky and there are not many clouds, the weather is hot and dry. If it is cloudy, the temperature will be lower.

Let the rain fall

Without water, there would be no life on Earth. Rain helps plants grow and gives animals water to drink.

temperature—*how hot or cold it is outside*

Icy water

Water freezes when it is
very cold. This changes
the weather. Snow falls
instead of rain, and water
on the ground turns into ice.

freezes—*turns into ice*

Our star

The Sun is a burning, hot star. It is so bright that it lights up Earth. The Sun also helps make our weather. It heats the land and air, making the wind blow, and it warms the oceans to make clouds and rain.

Night and day

Earth spins around once every 24 hours. When one side of Earth faces the Sun, it is daytime there. On the other side of the planet, it is nighttime.

spins—turns around

Sun worship

The Incas lived in South America many years ago. They worshipped the Sun. In those days, a lot of people thought that the Sun was a god because it was so powerful.

Burning heat

The Sun's rays can easily burn people's skin. Stay safe by covering up and using sunscreen. Never look directly at the Sun.

worship—*praying to something as a god*

Blanket of air

The atmosphere is a layer of air that covers Earth. It is where all weather happens. The atmosphere keeps our planet warm and protects it from dangers—such as being hit by space rocks.

Blue sky

The sky looks blue on a clear day. This is because of the way that sunlight shines through Earth's atmosphere.

protects—keeps safe from

Breathe in

The atmosphere is made up of a mixture of gases. Both plants and animals need these gases in order to stay alive.

Up and away

The atmosphere has five layers. The one closest to Earth is the troposphere. This is where clouds form. The layer farthest from Earth is the exosphere.

Layers of the atmosphere

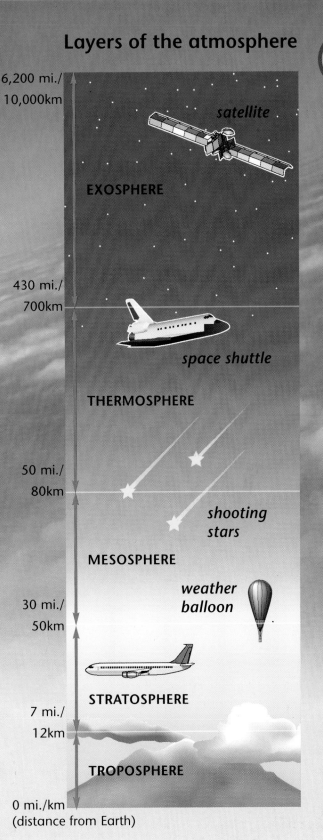

6,200 mi./ 10,000km

satellite

EXOSPHERE

430 mi./ 700km

space shuttle

THERMOSPHERE

50 mi./ 80km

shooting stars

MESOSPHERE

weather balloon

30 mi./ 50km

STRATOSPHERE

7 mi./ 12km

TROPOSPHERE

0 mi./km
(distance from Earth)

gases—*shapeless substances, such as air, that are not solid or liquid*

Changing seasons

Most countries have four seasons: winter, spring, summer, and fall. Seasons change because of the way that Earth orbits the Sun. Each orbit takes one year.

Earth on the move

Earth tilts, so each pole is closer to the Sun and is warmer at different times of the year. When it is summertime in the north, it is wintertime in the south.

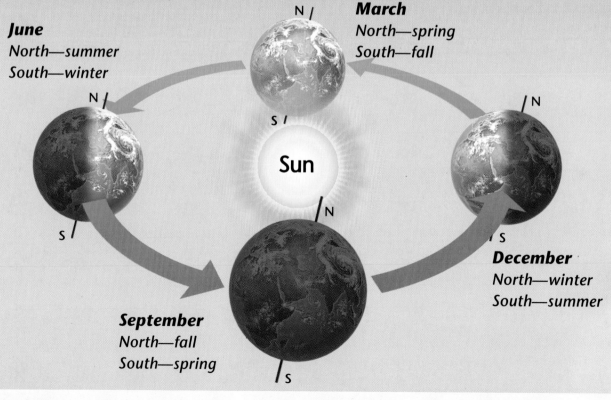

March
North—spring
South—fall

June
North—summer
South—winter

Sun

September
North—fall
South—spring

December
North—winter
South—summer

orbits—*moves around*

Spring and summer

In the spring, flowers bloom, and many animals have babies. The warmer weather of the summer follows the spring.

spring

Fall and winter

At the end of the summer, fall arrives, and the leaves drop off the trees. Then comes the chilly winter.

fall

pole—the point farthest north or farthest south on Earth

World climates

The normal weather that a place experiences is called its climate. There are different types of climates around the world. Some are hot and dry, while others are freezing cold or warm and wet.

Icy cold

Antarctica has the coldest climate on Earth. The emperor penguins that live there have blubber and special feathers to help them stay warm.

blubber—*a layer of fat*

Hot and dry

Deserts form where the climate is very dry and usually cloudless. They can change from sizzling hot during the day to freezing cold at night.

Warmed by the ocean

In Cornwall, England, there are palm trees, which usually only grow in hotter places. A warm sea current makes the climate there mild.

current—*a river of warmer or cooler water in an ocean*

(16) Blowing around

The air in the atmosphere is always on the move, blowing from one place to another. This is the wind. Some winds are only gentle breezes. Gales are strong winds that blow tiles off roofs—and people off their feet!

Weather vane
Whenever the wind blows a weather vane around, the arrow on it turns. The arrow stops once it points in the direction that the wind is blowing.

breezes—light, gentle winds

Flying kites

People have been flying
kites for thousands of years.
The wind lifts the kite, and
the owner can pull or steer
it with a long string.

steer—to move something one way or another

Wild wind

Strong winds can be very dangerous. They knock down buildings and injure people. But they are also useful— wind turbines can make electricity.

Dust storm

In places where the soil is dry, strong winds can create huge clouds of dust. These dust storms move quickly and can blow grit into our eyes, clothes, and hair.

wind turbines—*machines that turn in the wind*

Twisting wind

A tornado is a spinning funnel of wind that comes from a storm cloud. Some tornadoes are so powerful that they can suck a house right off the ground.

Whistling wind

The wind whistles when it blows hard through a small gap—like when someone whistles through their lips.

funnel—*a tube shape with a wider top and a narrower bottom*

Blue planet

Water covers most of Earth. As the Sun warms seas and lakes, it turns the water into vapor. Vapor is in the air, but it cannot be seen.

The water cycle

Water is always moving. When it rains, water falls into rivers, which flow into the sea. From there, the water turns into vapor and forms clouds. Then it rains again.

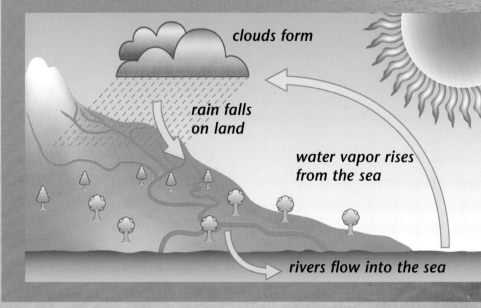

clouds form

rain falls
on land

water vapor rises
from the sea

rivers flow into the sea

vapor—water, mist, or fog in the atmosphere

Healthy water

Humans are also part of the water cycle. The water that we drink was once rain. People need to drink several glasses of water every day in order to stay healthy.

dolphins in the ocean

Enormous oceans

Oceans cover 72 percent of Earth's surface. They have a huge effect on our weather. Ocean currents carry warm, cold, or wet weather with them.

cycle—events that happen over and over again

Mist and clouds

Clouds can be made from tiny drops of water or from ice crystals. They are formed when warm air holding water vapor cools down. Clouds come in all shapes and sizes.

Fluffy cumulus

A cloud's name describes how high up it is in the sky and what it looks like. For example, the fluffy clouds seen during warm weather are called cumulus clouds.

crystals—tiny pieces of ice

Glowing at night

Some clouds glow in the dark, right after sunset. They look bright blue and are crisscrossed with wavy lines.

Tiger in the mist

Mist and fog are clouds that are close to the ground. They usually form during cool weather. This tiger's home in the jungle is very wet, so it is misty there, even though it is warm.

jungle—*a hot, wet place that is full of trees and plants*

Out in the rain

A raindrop is made when tiny drops of water in a cloud touch and join together. The raindrop gets larger and heavier, and finally it falls to the ground as rain.

The shape of rain

Rain may look like lines, but each raindrop is usually the shape of a sphere. Most are small— the size of a pencil tip.

sphere—a ball shape

Carried by the wind

Storms produce enormous, heavy raindrops. Strong winds keep the rain up in the air for a long time, so the drops get very big.

Leafy umbrella

Like humans, many animals like to shelter from the rain. Orangutans hold handfuls of leaves above their heads to stop them from getting wet.

produce—*to make*

Stormy days

A thunderstorm happens when clouds grow bigger and taller and gather more and more energy. Every day there can be as many as 40,000 storms crashing down around the world.

Lightning strikes

Lightning is a spark of electricity that makes the air glow. It can move between clouds or shoot down to the ground and onto trees or buildings.

energy—power, force

High as a mountain

Thunderclouds can be enormous. In very severe storms, they can be taller than a mountain!

Hurricane damage

A hurricane is a group of thunderstorms that spins around. In the middle is a calm circle called the eye. When a hurricane hits land, it can cause a lot of damage.

severe—*strong, powerful*

Wet and dry

Some parts of the world are rainy and wet. Other places are very dry. In deserts, years may pass without rain. But in the jungle, it can rain heavily all year long.

Pumping water

During a drought, there is not much rain. In very dry areas, people may have to walk to a well in order to get drinking water.

drought—when the weather is drier than normal

Water everywhere

When a lot of rain falls, it can cause floods. Floods are lakes of water that can cover a large area, even a whole city.

Dry land

When it does not rain for a long time, the ground can become so dry and hard that it cracks.

well—*a deep hole that leads to water under the ground*

Big freeze

When water gets very cold, it freezes into solid, slippery ice. You can see this as frost on plants and lawns or as a frozen, hard layer on a pond.

Handful of ice

Hailstones are balls of ice made in thunderclouds. They fall like rain, and the largest ones can be the size of a grapefruit. Ouch!

solid—*hard, not liquid*

Feathery crystals

Frost forms when air close to the ground is wet and so cold that it freezes. When it is warmer, this wetness makes dew instead.

Mountains of ice

Ice weighs less than water. This is why huge icebergs float. But only a small part of the ice can be seen. The rest is hidden underwater.

dew—*drops of water on, for example, grass, especially in the morning*

Flakes of snow

Snowflakes are made from ice that forms high up in the clouds. When it's warm out, the ice melts and falls to the ground as rain or sleet. If it is cold enough, it falls as snow.

Snowfall

Snowflakes are snow crystals that are stuck together. Big flakes form when the temperature is just below freezing. This is when the crystals are the stickiest.

sleet—*rain mixed with snow or hail*

Cozy snow

Snow can keep you warm!
The Inuit people, who live
in the Arctic, make
buildings called igloos
from blocks of snow.

Snow shapes

Most snow crystals have six sides,
but they never look exactly the
same as each other. They all form
different, beautiful patterns.

Arctic—the area around the North Pole

Light shows

Sometimes water and ice crystals can make light look very colorful or unusual. They can cause amazing things such as sun dogs and the beautiful, glowing light of a rainbow.

Colorful rainbow

When it rains and is sunny at the same time, it is sometimes possible to see a rainbow. A rainbow will be especially clear if a dark cloud lies behind the rain.

unusual—not common

Sun dogs

The two lights on both sides of the Sun are called sun dogs. They happen when sunlight shines through ice crystals in a particular way. They can have tails of light and look like dogs.

particular—special

Extreme weather

Sometimes the weather can be wild and dangerous. Hurricanes, floods, wildfires, and droughts are all types of extreme weather.

Waterpower

Floods may stretch over huge distances and cause a lot of damage. They can leave people stranded so that they need to be rescued by helicopter or boat.

Fighting fires

Wildfires break out in hot weather. This is because trees and plants dry out and then burn easily.

extreme—*the most unusual or severe*

El Niño

This is a current of warm
water in the Pacific Ocean
that happens every few years.
It can cause terrible floods,
droughts, and storms.

wildfires—*fires in forests or grasslands*

Rain or shine?

Weather forecasts tell us what the weather will be like for the next few days. Scientists use instruments and computers to make these forecasts.

Storm spotting

Trucks that have radar can find storms that are far away. Scientists then follow the storms and measure their strength.

Damp seaweed

There are easy ways to forecast the weather. For example, seaweed gets thick and floppy in wet air. This means that rain is coming.

instruments—tools that are used to take measurements

Weather balloons

Scientists use balloons
to lift instruments high up
into the sky. These then
measure the weather.

radar—an instrument that can locate objects that are far away

Future weather

Earth's climate naturally goes through times when it is a lot warmer or colder than it is today. However, many scientists believe that humans are changing the weather.

Smoky cars

The weather may be changing because of pollution. Pollution traps too much of the Sun's heat. This heat would normally escape into outer space.

pollution—harmful dirt such as smoke from cars

Getting warmer

Earth's climate is heating up. This makes ice melt and break away from icebergs and glaciers. As a result, the levels of the oceans rise and flood areas of land.

Help for farmers

Scientists are now better at forecasting weather several months ahead. Farmers use these forecasts to help them decide which crops to plant each year.

glaciers—solid rivers of ice

Making a kite

Kites soar in the sky because the wind pushes them upward. Decorate yours with an animal face—try a tiger!

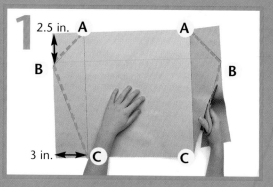

1 2.5 in. A   A
B   B
3 in. C   C

Following the measurements shown, on the piece of paper draw lines between A and C, A and B, and B and C. Cut the paper from C to B and B to A.

You will need

- Sheet of 11 x 17 paper
- Ruler
- Pencil
- Scissors
- Markers
- Tape
- Hole punch
- 2 long straws
- Colored tissue paper
- Thin string
- A thin stick

2 A   A
C   C

Turn the paper over and decorate your kite. You could draw a tiger. Make sure that A is at the top of the kite and C is at the bottom.

3 B   B

Put tape on the corners of the paper at B. Then use the hole punch to make holes through the tape, 1 in. from the edge, at B.

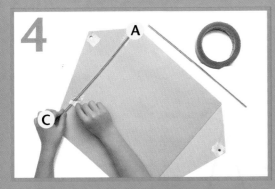

Turn the kite over. Use the tape to attach the straws on both sides of the paper along the lines between A and C.

Using the scissors, cut strips of colored tissue paper that are each 8 in. long. Tape the strips along the bottom edge of the kite.

Now your kite is ready to fly! Take a trip to the park and ask an adult to throw the kite high up into the air. Pull it along, holding tightly onto the stick.

Thread 30 in. of string through the punched-out holes and tie the ends together. The sides of the kite should bend inward slightly. Wind another long piece of string onto the stick. Tie the end to the middle of the string on the kite.

Sun dancer

Flashing lights

Your sun dancer will sparkle in the sunlight. If you place it near fruit bushes, it can help scare away birds and stop them from eating the berries.

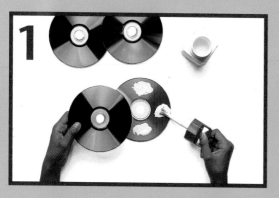

Place two CDs on a piece of paper with the shiny side facing down. Spread on some glue. Stick the CDs together. Leave them to dry. Repeat with the other CDs.

You will need

- 6 blank CDs
- Paper
- Glue for plastic/paper
- Shiny cardboard
- Pencil
- Scissors
- Thread (6 x 8 in., 2 x 10 in., 1 x 14 in.)
- String (14 in.)
- Small bells
- Stick (10 in.)

Draw six moons and six stars on the cardboard. Cut them out. Stick two star shapes together, with the shiny side out. Repeat with all of the shapes.

Ask an adult to make a small hole in the point of each star and moon. Poke 8 in. of thread through each hole and pull it halfway through.

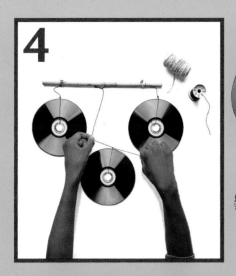

4

Tie the three longer pieces of thread to the stick, with the longest in the middle. Pull the end of each piece of thread through a CD and tie it tight to the top of the CD.

5

Add the moons, stars, and bells. These can be tied onto the thread and hung down from the CDs.

Tie the string onto the ends of the stick so that you can hang up your sun dancer. Place it by an open window or hang it in your yard. Watch it spin in the wind and dance in the sunlight.

Creating colors

Make a rainbow
See how water is able to split light into different colors and make an amazing rainbow at home.

You will need
- Glass jar
- Small mirror
- Flashlight
- Pitcher

Place the glass jar on a table in a room with plain, light-colored walls. Use the pitcher to fill the jar halfway with warm water.

Put the mirror in the jar and tilt it slightly upward. Close the curtains or blinds and turn off the light so that the room is very dark.

rainbow

Shine the flashlight on the mirror, and a rainbow should appear on the wall.

Swirling wind

Make a tornado

The swirling water in
this experiment acts like
the spinning wind of a
wild tornado.

You will need
- Big, plastic bottle with cap
- Dish liquid
- Food coloring
- Glitter

1

Fill the bottle with water and add
three drops of dish liquid and
some food coloring. Shake in
some glitter, which will act like
the dust that a tornado picks up.

tornado

*Screw the cap back on
tightly and then swirl your
bottle around in circles.
Put it down quickly and
watch what happens.*

Index

air 6, 8, 10–11, 16, 20, 22, 26
atmosphere 10–11, 16, 20
climate 14–15, 40, 41
clouds 6, 8, 18, 20, 22–23,
    24, 25, 26, 27, 30, 32, 34
crystals 22, 31, 32, 33,
    34, 35
currents 15, 21, 37
deserts 15, 28
dew 31
dolphins 21
droughts 28, 36, 37
Earth 6, 8, 10, 11, 12, 14,
    20, 21, 40, 41
El Niño 37
floods 29, 36, 37
fog 20, 23
frost 31
glaciers 41
hail and hailstones 30, 32
hurricanes 27, 36
ice 7, 22, 30–31, 32, 41
jungles 23, 28
light 34–35
lightning 26

mist 20, 22–23
oceans and seas 8, 15, 20, 21
orangutans 25
penguins 14
pollution 40
rain 6, 7, 8, 20, 21, 24–25,
    28, 29, 32, 34, 38
rainbows 34
seasons 12–13
sleet 32
snow 7, 12, 32–33
storms 18, 19, 25, 26–27,
    37, 38
Sun 6, 8–9, 12, 20, 35, 40
sun dogs 34, 35
temperature 6
thunderstorms 26–27
tigers 23
tornadoes 19
vapor 20, 22
water 6, 7, 20–21, 22, 28,
    30, 31, 34, 36, 37
weather forecasts 38–39, 41
wildfires 36, 37
wind 8, 16–17, 18–19, 25